Canadian ABC Adventures

Written by Claire Lemieux
Illustrated by Marilyn Mets

Troll Associates

Printed in Canada.

10 9 8 7 6 5 4 3 2

Aa

A is for Alberta,
where the mountains meet the plains.

Bb

B is for beaver building a dam.

Cc Dd

C is for caribou, who roam the land.
D is for Douglas Fir, growing tall and proud.

Ee

E is for Ellesmere Island,
as far north as you can go.

Ff

F is for the many forests where the animals play.

Gg Hh

G is for goose who sits by the pond.
H is for hockey, our national sport.

Ii

I is for Inuit, natives of the north.

Jj

J is for Jasper National Park,
a place of beauty and peace.

Kk Ll

K is for kayak, gliding down the river.
L is for loon, diving into the water.

Mm

M is for moose, the largest of the deer family.

Nn

N is for Nova Scotia, where the fishermen set sail.

Oo

O is for Ottawa, our capital city.

Pp

P is for prairie, the French word for "meadow."

Qq

Q is for Quebec,
Algonquin for "where the river narrows."

Rr

R is for Rocky Mountains,
home to five national parks.

Ss Tt

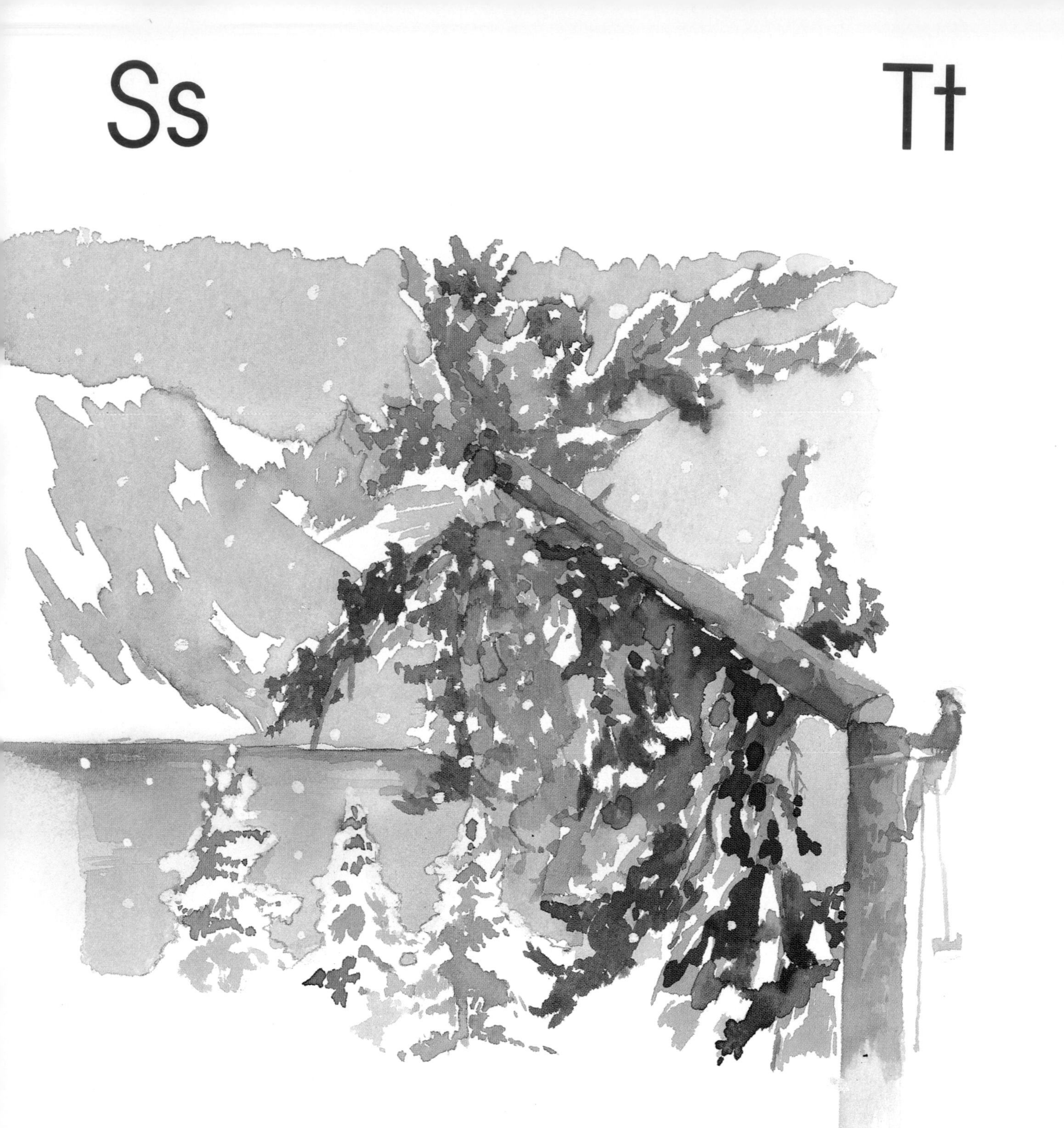

S is for snow that blankets the cold north.
T is for "TIMBER!" as a tree comes down.

Uu

U is for uniform worn by the
Royal Canadian Mounted Police.

Vv

V is for Victoria,
where we ride a double-decker bus.

Ww

W is for whale watchers in a big boat.

Xx

X is for the "x" in Halifax,
the capital of Nova Scotia.

Yy

Y is for Yellowknife, a cold city in the north.

Zz

Z is for zoo. Is there one near you?